Original title:
Trellis of Dreams

Copyright © 2025 Creative Arts Management OÜ
All rights reserved.

Author: Giselle Montgomery
ISBN HARDBACK: 978-1-80567-070-4
ISBN PAPERBACK: 978-1-80567-150-3

The Unfolding of Timeless Whispers

In a garden of giggles, the flowers jest,
They swap silly secrets, and never rest.
Bumblebees buzz with a comedic flair,
Tickling the daisies, floating in air.

A squirrel in shades does a dance by the oak,
Cracking up rabbits with each funny joke.
They roll on the grass, clutching their sides,
As the wise old owl hoots, and joy abides.

The sunbeams tickle the leaves, oh so bright,
While shadows shimmy in the warm sunlight.
A lizard in a top hat struts down the path,
Chasing his tail, igniting some laughs.

Stars join the chorus, a twinkling band,
Winking at night, with a giggle so grand.
In this whimsical world where all is a jest,
Laughter grows wild, and we are all blessed.

Fences of Fate

Where squirrels plot their little schemes,
And birds dance in their silly teams,
The fence post wobbles in the breeze,
While grasshoppers play tag with ease.

A hedgehog dons a tiny hat,
Declaring war on one fat rat,
The daisies giggle, what a sight,
As twilight falls, they sing with delight.

Serenade of Solitary Stars

Oh lonely star who twirls alone,
While planets laugh and share their tone,
You'd think they'd send a little light,
To keep you company at night.

A comet swings by, tips its hat,
And off it zooms, just like a cat,
While asteroids tap to a beat,
The universe grooves—oh what a feat!

Weaving the Fabric of Belief

With threads of doubt and hope entwined,
A tapestry of quirks designed,
Each stitch a chuckle, plucked with glee,
As laughter bounds like a bumblebee.

We knit our wishes, loop by loop,
In crazy patterns, jump and droop,
A patchwork quilt of dreams so bright,
That tickles all who glimpse its light.

Boundless Blooms of the Mind

In gardens where the jesters play,
And candy clouds drift into sway,
The daisies twist in jest so sweet,
As butterflies break out in beat.

A dandelion with flair so bold,
Whispers secrets, tales retold,
While petunias giggle, side by side,
As silly thoughts begin to glide.

The Framework of Forgotten Pathways

Beneath the leaves, a whispered jest,
The squirrels debate, who is the best.
One claims acorns, the other, pears,
Yet all they find are lost lovers' stares.

Paths once bright, now tangled and steep,
Even the grass rolls in its sleep.
A map upside down, on wild dog's back,
They plot their course, but lose the track.

Echoes of Untold Stories

Loud laughter springs from a hollow log,
Where frogs wear crowns, but only on fog.
They croak tales of knights in muddy shoes,
And waltz with the dragonflies, sharing the blues.

Along the creek where shadows dance,
The fish swap gags, given half a chance.
But the wise old turtle just shakes his head,
While munching on lettuce, confused but fed.

Spheres of Serenity and Splendor

In gardens where wisps of whimsy weave,
The bees wear bow ties on each fine eve.
Butterflies giggle, in colors galore,
Competing for laughs, like a comedy store.

A snail, in his shell, seeks fashion advice,
While crickets debate, who's the best at dice.
Each bloom is a stage for a hilarious tale,
Where even the weeds get up to regale.

Interlaced Dreams of the Soul

As moonbeams knit the stars with a grin,
The owls host parties where night critters spin.
Raccoons in tuxedos steal pies at the feast,
While fireflies flash as a sparkly beast.

In the depths of the night, all worries are far,
As the cats plot heists beneath the bright star.
With laughter and mischief, they gather around,
In dreams woven tightly, where joy can be found.

The Secret Garden of Tomorrow

In a garden where the gnomes dance,
Funny hats twirl with a whimsical chance.
Flowers giggle when the sun hits right,
Spreading laughter through the moonlit night.

Butterflies play hide and seek with bees,
As squirrels plot to steal the leaves with ease.
A rabbit wears glasses, looks quite posh,
While ivy listens, laughing in a nosh.

A Symphony of Flawed Perfections

A cat on a piano sings out of tune,
While mice in tuxedos dance under the moon.
Each wrong note is simply a silly prank,
As cacti play harmonicas down by the bank.

Chickens in choirs squawk rhythmically loud,
Joining the hedgehogs, all feeling quite proud.
Together they make a comical scene,
In a concert that's nothing short of serene.

Dreams That Shimmer in Twilight

Stars pop like popcorn in the evening sky,
While dreams ride bicycles, zipping by.
Each thought wears a tutu, a twinkly flair,
Floating on clouds, without a single care.

A jester's hat teeter-totters with glee,
As fireflies giggle, buzzing with the spree.
Together they dance to a melody sweet,
In a land where silly is the grandest feat.

Seeds of Change in Gentle Winds

Seeds float on breezes, wearing tiny crowns,
While squirrels swap gossip in fluffy brown gowns.
Each whisper transforms into giggling sprout,
As dandelions plot to turn the world out.

A parade of frogs hops down the lane,
Wearing little boots, causing a sweet strain.
With patches of laughter stitched into their days,
They trendily march in peculiar ballet.

Shadows Cast by Wishes

In the garden of thoughts we roam,
Duck-taped dreams will find a home.
Jellybeans dance on a moonlit night,
While rubber ducks prepare for flight.

Gorillas play chess under the stars,
And tumbleweeds spin tales of cars.
This silly world, a laugh-filled stage,
Where whimsies leap from page to page.

Arbors of Aspirations

In a tree where wishes hang,
Dancing squirrels start to sang.
Pine cones fall like popcorn treats,
As laughter echoes 'round our feet.

A butterfly's a savvy thief,
He swipes dreams like they're a leaf.
While ants in tuxedos march on by,
Claiming the throne, oh my, oh my!

Canopy of Colors Unseen

Under this shade of polka dots,
Painted dreams fill empty spots.
Cupcakes rain down like confetti,
While chairs do cha-chas, bright and petty.

Wiggly worms sing in a band,
With spoons as instruments, oh so grand.
A rainbow spills from a jellyfish's hat,
And giggles echo from a chatting cat.

The Framework of Tomorrow

Tomorrow's house is built on fun,
With bubble wrap roofs kissed by the sun.
Each wall covered in sketches bright,
A trampoline jumps to greet the night.

Bees in tuxes buzz out their plans,
While carrots juggle in their stands.
A squirrel offers tips on flight,
As dreams take off into the night.

Blossoms in a Forgotten Garden

In a garden where crickets dance,
Daisies wear hats, join the prance.
The roses grumble, 'We're not that sweet!'
While sunflowers nod to the rhythm of feet.

A squirrel forgot where it hid its stash,
While tulips giggle—oh what a clash!
Lettuce whispers, 'Is it time for tea?'
Cucumbers comment, 'Oh, let's just be!'

Leaves Beneath a Starlit Sky

Under stars that twinkle and wink,
Leaves gossip about how to drink.
A squirrel in pajamas climbs high with flair,
While roots rave about the soil's fair share.

Crickets chirp of the latest trends,
As mushrooms argue, 'Are we friends?'
The moon winks at the leafy crowd,
And laughter erupts, boisterous and loud!

Pathways of Desires

In a maze of paths where dreams collide,
A garden gnome takes a bumpy ride.
He claims his map leads to hidden gold,
But all he finds is a marigold, bold.

Butterflies chase after the whims of fate,
While ants declare, 'We're feeling great!'
A ladybug laughs, 'Oh, let's not race!'
In this garden, we all find our place.'

The Grid of Glimmering Future

In a web of plans, robots debate,
Should we dance, or should we wait?
A toaster dreams of being a star,
While the blender just wants to go far!

Neon lights buzz with electric glee,
As microwaves say, 'What's next for me?'
The calendar laughs, 'It's almost time!'
To celebrate with a dance and a rhyme!'

The Web of Aspirations

In a world where wishes fly,
I found a kite stuck in the sky.
My hopes are tangled in its strings,
And all it does is flap and sing.

At breakfast, dreams float in my cup,
I sip on clouds and giggle up.
My toast is crispy, just like my goals,
But jelly spills, and laughter rolls.

Each ambition dances on a line,
Some more wobbly than fine wine.
I try to climb my ladder high,
But trip on shoelaces, oh my, oh my!

Waltzing with whims on a sunny day,
Chasing the squirrels that dart and play.
Life's a circus! Come join the fun,
Bicycles and bananas? Oh, just one!

Secrets Woven in Stardust

In a loom of glitter and cheeky mess,
Fabrics weave tales of silliness.
A unicorn pranced with a polka dot tie,
While shooting stars winked from the pie in the sky.

I brewed a potion of giggles and glee,
With unicorn hair, just for me!
But bubblegum stuck to my shoe,
And frogs croaked out 'Just kiss us too!'

Behind the curtain, dreams wear hats,
A raccoon plays chess with the old house cats.
With every quilt, laughter unfolds,
And secrets in stardust never get old.

So sing with the moon and dance at dawn,
In this silly world, we'll carry on.
Woven in stardust, we all will shine,
With not a single wrinkle or line!

Blooming Through the Night

Petals giggle in the evening breeze,
Flowers chime in their shoes, oh please!
Dancing daisies tip-toe around,
While crickets play hopscotch on the ground.

Under the moon, the marigolds grin,
They've had too much laughter and gin.
Tulips whisper knock-knock jokes,
And the night air fills with playful pokes.

Oh, blooming is such a funny affair,
With garden gnomes just chilling there.
They laugh so hard, they almost drop,
Their tiny hats—they just can't stop!

So come join the plants in their delight,
As they bloom and joke through the night.
In this garden, every dream is bright,
With leaves that giggle till morning light!

Echoes of Tomorrow's Light

Whispers travel through the day's good cheer,
Tickling toes with a giggle, my dear.
Tomorrow plans a funny parade,
With silly hats and a marching brigade.

Clouds giggle as raindrops fall,
They bump and bounce off the garden wall.
Laughter echoes through every street,
With a squirrel in lederhosen, so neat!

Chasing echoes with dreams in tow,
It's a wobbly ride, but go, go, go!
With balloon animals dancing about,
And silly faces that shimmer and shout.

So wave to the echoes of future delight,
As they bounce from shadows into the light.
Life's a carnival—so join the fray,
With laughter and joy leading the way!

Canvases of Celestial Wishes

In galaxies bright, we ride on a cat,
With wishes so wild, like a fanciful hat.
Jupiter laughs with a wink in his eye,
While Mars plays the kazoo as the moon says bye.

Stars drop their paint, a comical spree,
Dancing in circles, as happy as can be.
Aliens join in with a soft shoe glide,
Creating a canvas where chaos won't hide.

The Embrace of Growing Glories

Flowers wear sunglasses, soaking in sun,
While daisies throw parties, oh what fun!
Roses attempt to perform tap dance,
While tulips stand guard, giving no chance.

Vines chuckle softly, they tango with glee,
As greenery whispers, "Come join the spree!"
Fruity confetti falls from this green lair,
Nature's embrace is a wacky affair!

The Maze of Hopes and Yearnings

In a maze of mischief, where dreams collide,
We take brave steps, with gumballs as our guide.
Bouncing around corners, with silliness keen,
Chasing down wishes, in spaces unseen.

Cowlicks of hope twist in playful delight,
We stumble on wishbones, laughing outright.
The walls gently chuckle, the path's never straight,
As we skip through the maze, it's a whimsical fate!

Enchanted Frameworks of the Heart

Frames of odd shapes, they shimmy and sway,
With laughter that echoes in a kooky ballet.
Hearts dressed in sequins perform with delight,
In corners of whimsy, they twinkle so bright.

Balloons in a chorus, sing songs of romance,
While ribbons do the cha-cha, they prance and dance.
As love twirls around in these frames made of fun,
Every heartbeat echoes, two usually one.

Serendipity in the Canvas Sky

Balloons that float, oh what a sight,
Chasing after clouds, with all my might.
A cat on a skateboard, how peculiar,
Grinning at me, oh, this is a thrill!

Jellybeans rain, a colorful spree,
Umbrellas are flipping, just wait and see.
Sunflowers giggle, they dance in the breeze,
Whispering secrets, oh, what a tease!

Kites made of pizza, they soar and glide,
While bears on bicycles take each wild ride.
Tickles from raindrops, laughter in air,
Serendipity feasting without a care!

Stars wearing glasses, twinkling, they wink,
Cupcakes in dreams, don't you love to blink?
Silly delight hides in each twist and turn,
Sometimes it's magic, oh, how we learn.

Dreamscapes of Lost Letters

A postman in flip-flops, surfing on mail,
Each envelope giggles, none can curtail.
Written in whispers, the words play a game,
Sending love notes, each one looks the same.

Socks in a drawer hold secrets so grand,
They argue and bicker, forming a band.
Mysteries wrapped in a rainbow of cloth,
Dancing alongside a mischievous moth!

Messages floating on waves of sweet air,
Comets delivering tales, quite rare.
Postcards from fairies, they slide through the night,
Their giggles echoing, what a delight!

Ink spills like secrets, across patterned sky,
Every letter a treasure that dares to fly.
Dreams collected, like stamps in a book,
Each one a journey; oh, take a look!

The Dance of Flickering Lights

Fireflies flapping in synchrony bright,
A waltz in the shadows, oh what a sight!
Lanterns are laughing, swaying with glee,
They twinkle like stars, just wait and see!

One lamp has a crush on the moon up above,
Winking and giggling, oh what's with love?
Twisting and twirling, oh how they glide,
In the darkened corners, they know where to hide.

Neon signs whisper jokes from the street,
Mixing up colors, oh what a feat!
Flickering candles, with secrets to share,
Each laugh and chuckle spins in the air.

A chandelier chuckles, it jiggles in place,
Glittering memories all over the space.
The dance of the lights, oh what a delight,
Tickling laughter, a marvelous night!

Carving Pathways in the Ether

Clouds like marshmallows, soft and so sweet,
Riding on rainbows, what a fun feat.
Silly squirrels plotting a heist in the night,
Stealing the moon, oh what a delight!

Stardust is sprinkled on all we can see,
As they giggle and tumble, oh so carefree.
Chasing horizons where giggles can roam,
Each twist of the pathway feels just like home.

Whimsical whispers float through the air,
Twirling like fairies without any care.
Mapping the cosmos with crayons so bright,
Carving out pathways, oh what a sight!

Giggles intertwine, with dreams in their wake,
A tapestry woven, no heart can forsake.
In the ether we dance, with joy on our feet,
Carving out laughter, so wild and sweet!

A Tangle of Thoughts and Fantasies

In a garden where thoughts get tangled,
Silly ideas dance, a bit wrangled.
A cat in a hat with a whimsical grin,
Sips on the sun as the day begins.

The flowers wear shoes made of candy,
While butterflies plan parties quite dandy.
A frog plays the lute, what a silly sight,
As the moon chuckles down through the night.

Clouds take a stroll, with no place to go,
Juggling the raindrops, putting on a show.
The trees tell jokes, oh, what a delight,
In a tangle of thoughts that take flight.

If daydreams were money, we'd all be quite rich,
But we trip on our thoughts, like a welcoming hitch.
We'll laugh at the world while we twirl and sway,
In this zany garden where dreams come to play.

The Archway to Possibilities

Through an archway of whimsy, I skip and I prance,
Where squirrels wear suits and invite you to dance.
A hedgehog in glasses reads stories in rhyme,
As carrots join hands and form a conga line.

Beneath an umbrella that twirls in the sky,
Raindrops tap dance as they drift on by.
Each step brings a giggle, each turn a surprise,
With balloons for companions, laughter never dies.

A rabbit with dreams, he navigates fate,
Stumbles on cake, and says, "What a weight!"
But don't mind the mess, it's all part of fun,
As we leap through the archway, we're never done.

With each twist and turn, possibilities bloom,
In this wacky realm where we dance through the gloom.
So come take a chance, let your worries release,
Join the parade of laughter and endless peace.

Tendrils of Tomorrow

In the garden of giggles, tomorrow sprouts wide,
With tendrils of silly, they twist and they slide.
A cucumber smiles, wears a top hat with style,
As the sun tickles daisies, brightening the mile.

There's a worm on a skateboard, rushes past me,
Screaming and laughing, "Just wait until three!"
The daisies join in for a bright dance-off,
As the ants take the stage, and begin to scoff.

With popcorn clouds fluffing in cottony air,
We ride on the breeze without any care.
The grasshoppers chirp out a beat for the day,
While shadows perform on the sidewalk ballet.

With the roots of tomorrow wrapping dreams all around,
We'll leap over puddles of giggles unbound.
So gather your wishes, they're ripe for the night,
In a whirl of tomorrow, we'll soar out of sight.

The Secret Garden of Yearning

In a secret spot where oddities bloom,
The flowers gossip, dispelling all gloom.
A dragon that sneezes makes rainbows so bright,
And starfish in tuxedos dance under the light.

Gnomes teach the squirrels how to play chess,
While frogs serve fresh pies, oh what a mess!
Each whispering breeze shares a tale that's absurd,
With laughter that lingers, such joy can be heard.

The leaves wear great hats, and the sun is a friend,
As dreams frolic freely, they twist and they bend.
In this secret garden, a giggle is gold,
Where wishes are tangled in stories retold.

Let's pluck our desires and let them take flight,
With a sprinkle of humor to guide us tonight.
In the garden of yearning, we'll make merry cheer,
Crafting laughter and dreams that will last all year.

Woven Whispers of Hope

In a garden where giggles sprout,
A tomato wearing a sun hat shouts.
"If you want to grow, just laugh and sway,
We'll dance through night, then greet the day!"

A cucumber claims it's a pirate's glee,
Swashbuckling dreams in our veggie spree.
With zucchinis rolling like playful pup,
We'll harvest joy and never give up!

Beans gossip loud, spread tales far and wide,
As peas join in, with a joyful ride.
A salad party under the moon's glow,
With dressing so tangy, it steals the show!

So come plant laughter, let the fun ensue,
In this patch of whimsy, there's joy for you.
Weaving stories, in rows, we play,
In a garden of chuckles, we'll forever stay!

Climbing Hearts in the Twilight

As night falls, the stars start to climb,
A banana peels jokes, one at a time.
"Why did the berry blush into pink?
It saw the grape slip, and really did wink!"

With shadows that dance like a comical crew,
The pumpkins gather for a jolly view.
"Let's roll ourselves, down this hill so steep,
And laugh so loud, we might wake the sheep!"

Each twinkling light brings a whimsy to share,
A squash with a top hat, full of flair.
"I juggle my dreams, like balls in the air,
A squash cabaret, we'll dance without care!"

So raise your glasses, with fruits on display,
In twilight's embrace, we'll laugh and play.
With climbing hearts, we'll echo the night,
Where silly moments make everything right!

Lattice of Longing

Amidst the lattice, where giggles reside,
A honeybee buzzes, with prideful glide.
"Why hum so softly? Let's raise a cheer!
I've got the best pollen, come gather near!"

The daisies are dancing, twirling about,
While the roses just grin, no room for doubt.
"We're on a mission, to fill up the air,
With laughter and joy, not a single care!"

Each vine has a secret, each petal a plan,
The lilacs gossip, it's all part of the clan.
"What's the buzz, my friend? You look quite bemused!
Join our flower show, you'll see it's enthused!"

As stars peek through, a whimsical night,
With dreams interwoven, so fluffy and bright.
In this garden of laughter, our wishes take flight,
Where longing for joy makes everything light!

Vines of Vision

The vines are scheming, with visions so clear,
A radish declares, "Let's spread some cheer!
With dreams in the soil, and a twinkling root,
We'll grow a parade in our best veggie suit!"

A pumpkin rolls over, with a chuckle so grand,
"With friends by my side, I can take any stand!
Let's hop through the fields, and sing through the nights,
Create silly shadows with whimsical lights!"

Each cucumber whispers a story or two,
As carrots giggle at the sky's sparkling hue.
"We'll climb up the fence, just to see the show,
Where dreams mix with laughter, like a comedy glow!"

So join this adventure where vines intertwine,
In gardens of humor, life's simply divine.
With vision of joy in each little sprout,
We'll chase after laughter, there's never a doubt!

Chamber of Echoing Fantasies

In halls where giggles never fade,
A jester's hat is proudly displayed.
Each corner whispers silly schemes,
While laughter bounces off our dreams.

A cat in shoes, the stars align,
As unicorns sip tea and dine.
The walls are painted poppy red,
With bubblegum clouds above our head.

A pirate's parrot cracks a joke,
While mermaids dance and softly poke.
The floorboards creak with playful glee,
As we all share our zany spree.

In this strange place where fun takes flight,
We spin and twirl till day turns night.
With every echo, joy returns,
As laughter in our hearts still burns.

The Bridge Between Now and Forever

A bridge that wobbles, bounces, sways,
Where turtles race and people play.
With cotton candy clouds above,
And butterflies that coo of love.

Each step we take, a giggle grows,
With dancing shoes and silly clothes.
A frog on stilts jumps high with grace,
While fish in hats join in the race.

The trolls below just roll their eyes,
At laughter loud as squeaky pies.
They huff and puff, try to complain,
But we just leap and dance again.

As sunsets streak the sky with cheer,
We wave to time, there's nothing to fear.
The bridge will bend, but never break,
For each new step, a fun mistake.

Vines of Hope and Resilience

In gardens where the wild vines climb,
They tickle noses, one at a time.
With leaves like hands that wave hello,
And giggles springing free to flow.

A gnome in shorts tends to the plot,
While squirrels debate the best-shaped pot.
They dig for treasure—candy, not gold,
As stories of wacky spoons are told.

The sun throws down its warm embrace,
While flowers dance and do the chase.
Each petal flutters, trying to sing,
A tune about the joy of spring.

So here we grow, in laughter's shade,
With hope that never, ever fades.
Together we'll face what may come,
Turning brave tales to joyful hum.

Currents of Untold Journeys

On waves of whimsy, boats set sail,
With frogs and cats, they tell the tale.
A cactus captain leads the way,
As stars above begin to play.

Seas of giggles splash with glee,
While octopuses dance with glee.
The wind whispers secrets, laughs out loud,
As jellyfish twirl like they're proud.

We navigate through dream-like lands,
Where candy canes grow in the sands.
Each island hides a silly knave,
With treasure chests of joy to save.

So gather 'round, come take a ride,
On currents where the fun won't hide.
With maps that fold in quirky ways,
We'll sail forever, fueled by plays.

An Odyssey of Wispy Whispers

In the garden of thoughts, quite absurd,
A snail wrote a novel, it was unheard.
With a pen made of lettuce, oh what a sight,
It published its saga one snail-paced night.

A fish claimed it swam in a poet's flair,
Telling tales of bubbles, light as air.
The clouds laughed aloud, a drizzling jest,
While dreams did a jig in their fanciest vest.

The moon wore a hat, quite tall and round,
With stars in its pockets, sparkling profound.
It waltzed with the night, in a tango of dreams,
While the world spun in giggles, or so it seems.

A squirrel recited in a wobbly tone,
Poetry brushed with acorn and bone.
And all who heard chuckled, what a parade,
In this zany ballet where nonsense was made.

The Merging of Mindscapes

In a land where thoughts play hopscotch with time,
A cactus danced tango, it was sublime.
With shoes made of rainbows, so vivid, so bright,
It jived with a mountain, a curious sight.

A cat wore a tie, with stripes and a flair,
Declaring its café was the best in the air.
The mice were the waiters, quite nimble and spry,
Serving cheese-flavored lattes, oh me, oh my!

A parrot was singing in tones so bizarre,
About love lost to tacos from a distant star.
The planets giggled, swaying left and right,
As costumes of laughter adorned the night.

In the chaos of whimsy, reality bends,
Where the quirk of each moment merrily blends.
Each thought, a balloon, floating high, full of glee,
In this fiesta of craziness, wild and free.

Lullabies in a Field of Wishes

Beneath the moon's grin, a rabbit sang low,
About dreams that sprouted like corn in a row.
It swayed with the daisies, oh what a delight,
As wishes took flight on a breeze of the night.

A unicorn juggled some stars in a hat,
While squirrels debated the worth of a spat.
With giggles like sparkling, sweet sugar for tea,
The fireflies danced with a glow, so carefree.

A frog turned philosopher, wise as could be,
Claiming ponds were portals to wild jubilee.
With ripples of laughter, the night softly spun,
As wishes and whims began joining for fun.

The lullabies echoed through soft autumn haze,
With each note a promise of mischievous days.
In this meadow of mirth, all their dreams took flight,
In a symphony stitched from the fabric of night.

Harmonies of a Hopeful Heart

In a world of sweet giggles, a dreamer did twirl,
Wearing socks made of clouds, with a grin and a whirl.
It painted the sky with crayons and cheer,
As rainbows joined hands, drawing laughter near.

A gnome with a kazoo led a parade,
Of mushrooms and daisies that merrily played.
With spiders as drummers, they tapped on the leaves,
Creating a symphony that nobody believes.

A llama in glasses read poems to trees,
While branches applauded with rustling leaves.
The grass waved its arms in a jovial stance,
In this carnival land, where whimsy could dance.

As stars punctuated the deep velvet night,
Each twinkle a chuckle, each shimmer a flight.
In this hopeful embrace, where joy plays its part,
They found all their smiles in the beats of the heart.

A Mosaic of Quiet Longings

In a garden of whims, cats chase the sun,
Sipping the dew, oh, what a fun run!
They plot and they plan for a milk-filled feast,
As birds chirp loudly, they dance like a beast.

With dreams made of yarn, they tangle with glee,
Creating a ruckus, oh let it be free!
But who will untie these knots in the night?
Maybe a dog, with dreams taking flight.

In shadows they leap, like stars on a spree,
Twirling with laughter, what a sight to see!
The moon winks down, with no care in sight,
For dreams made of laughs are the best ones, right?

Each crack of the dawn brings the end of the play,
But wait! Is that toast with some jam on display?
As visions dissolve, with each bite, they know,
The crazy adventures are sure to flow!

Serenity in Painted Skies

Brush strokes of clouds in a canvas of blue,
A duck on a skateboard, who knew it could do?
It quacks out a tune, much to everyone's cheer,
The sun giggles softly, it's happy out here.

Pigeons do pirouettes on the very next swing,
While squirrels in tuxedos plan a grand fling.
They dream of a nut ball, elegant and fine,
With acorn confetti and drinks made of wine.

The sky blushes pink, with a hint of delight,
As shadows embrace the fading daylight.
Our laughter floats up where the twinkling stars beam,
Crafting a quilt of the silliest dream.

In this painted expanse, let's dance and let's shout,
For the world's just a stage where we paint in and out.
With whimsies and giggles, we color the night,
Making memories sparkle, oh what a sweet sight!

Lanterns Guiding Untrodden Paths

With lanterns aglow, they venture afar,
Frogs sing in harmony, a bright little guitar.
The path twists and bends, full of mischief and glee,
With shadows that giggle, come take a look-see!

A hedgehog in glasses reads stories of space,
While bunnies on pogo sticks bounce all over the place.
The owls hoot in laughter as they watch the parade,
While fireflies dance like a glowing charade.

Each glow tells a joke, with the moon as a host,
A comedy night that no one can boast.
The night holds a magic that's wonderfully funny,
With laughter that echoes, not needing any money.

So follow the lights, and let your joy flow,
In a world where silliness continues to grow.
These lanterns will guide you to dreams that are sweet,
Where fun and adventure are always a treat!

The Veil Between Reality and Desire

In the land where socks dance and slippers delight,
Tigers wear polka dots, oh, what a sight!
A world made of giggles and pies in the sky,
Where ice cream is solid, and clouds never cry.

Beneath the soft whispers of wishes and whim,
A turtle in sunglasses teaches us to swim.
He glides through the waves with an ease so divine,
While fish perform ballet, oh how they entwine!

Each wish on a star takes an unusual twist,
With gnarly green monsters who cannot resist.
They skateboard on rainbows, and sing in high pitch,
Chasing down dreams with a zany old hitch.

So tiptoe through veils; embrace every cheer,
Life's quirks are just treasures that make it all clear.
When laughter blooms loud, and dreams intertwine,
Reality winks, saying, "You'll be just fine!"

Portals to the Unknown

In a garden where gnomes play hide and seek,
They sip on tea, and giggle, not meek.
A cat in a hat jogs with a grin,
Chasing butterflies, oh where to begin?

The flowers debate, who smells the best,
While worms in the soil plan their little fest.
A snail with a shell that's painted bright,
Claims he's the fastest, what a silly sight!

In the shadows, the fairies all dance,
Winking at crickets while taking a chance.
The moon's got a wink, wearing shades of blue,
Oh, what a riot, this world that we drew!

So tread lightly here, in this jolly place,
Where laughter echoes, in every space.
With portals that swirl and twirl oh so round,
Grab your markers, let joy be found!

Enchanted Eclipses

When the sun and the moon decide to collide,
They form a sandwich, with starry pride.
The sprightly squirrels cheer from the tree,
While bounce in their step is a sight to see.

The chipmunks wear capes, spreading delight,
As shadows grow silly in the soft moonlight.
A dance-off erupts with the stars on cue,
Who knew the cosmos could be such a zoo?

The clouds are the judges, with popcorn in tow,
Rating each spin, each twirl, and each blow.
A comet zooms by, sporting glasses of red,
In this kooky show, anything's said!

As laughter resounds, like ripples in breeze,
The night wears a smile, full of gentle tease.
In these eclipses of whimsy, let's take a claim,
To joy and to giggles, oh what a game!

Leaves of Perception Falling

In a forest of whimsy where wishes take flight,
Leaves whisper secrets, with colors so bright.
A beetle with boots leads a laughable trot,
Surveying the world, it's a merry old plot.

The owls wear glasses, reading the news,
While raccoons in coats sip on fruity brews.
A squirrel recites lines from an old fable,
While eagles bring snacks, all set on a table.

As leaves tumble down like confetti in fall,
The trees stand up tall, giggling for all.
With each little plop, the laughter grows loud,
In this playful scene, let's gather a crowd!

So join the parade of the silly and free,
Where imagination flows like a jubilant spree.
With leaves of perception, let's play and explore,
In this dance of discovery, we always want more!

Evergreen Echoes of Serenity

In a forest of giggles, the tall trees tease,
With branches that sway in the light, oh so pleased.
The pinecones are poets, with verses quite tall,
Reciting their rhymes for the critters' grand ball.

A fox in a bow tie hosts this wild show,
While birds in sleek tuxedos steal the next row.
The rabbits do cartwheels, flipping with flair,
But oops! Someone tripped—what a tumble in air!

Underneath the stars, they dance 'neath the moon,
In a rhythm so sunny, it ends far too soon.
The echoes of laughter roll soft through the night,
In this vibrant refuge, everything's right.

So gather your friends, let the merriment soar,
In the evergreen echoes, there's always room for more.
Where serenity tickles and joy sprinkles light,
Join in the fun, it's a beautiful sight!

Fragments of a Dreamer's Canvas

A painter's brush is quite absurd,
It splatters colors—not a word!
The canvas giggles, takes a glance,
As peanut butter starts to dance.

A splish, a splash, a twisty stroke,
With ramen noodles, dreams awoke!
A turtle in a top hat grins,
And all at once, the fun begins.

Bright oranges and polka dots,
A llama laughing at the knots.
Each blob a wish, just floating free,
In this wild world of make-believe.

Oh, paint me skies of lemon zest,
Where jellybeans frolic with the best!
With every drip and every glint,
Life's just a joke—and isn't that the hint?

Poems Beneath the Blossoming Sky

Beneath the clouds of cotton candy,
A squirrel wrote a sonnet dandy!
With acorns dropped like clapping hands,
The whole park's caught in silly bands.

A flower sneezed, and pollen flew,
As bees did tango, who knew?!
The trees wore hats of neon green,
And every branch joined in the scene.

Sipping nectar, flowers twirl,
While ladybugs in waltz do whirl.
The bees, they buzz a goofy tune,
While clouds applaud, it's quite the boon!

Oh dance with me 'neath skies so vast,
We'll plant some dreams that grow so fast.
With roots of laughter in the air,
This blooming jest is beyond compare!

The Radiance of Uncultivated Thoughts

In gardens where the wild thoughts play,
A crow recites a haiku each day.
With topsy-turvy, twisty bends,
A tumbleweed that makes amends.

Thoughts bloom like mushrooms in the dark,
While squirrels plot a secret park.
With giggles chirping from the vines,
Uncultivated, laughter shines!

A gopher with a monocle found,
Designs his house so underground.
The daffodils don't look so neat,
As thoughts take shape on wobbly feet.

Let's toast our dreams with fizzy pop,
In this wild garden, never stop!
For every quirk and zany scheme,
Is just a thread in life's funny seam.

A Patchwork of Daring Dreams

In a quilt of giggles, brightly sewn,
A cat in pajamas starts to groan.
With button eyes, it dreams away,
Of chasing fish that like to play.

Each stitch a story, bold and strange,
From unicorns to cowboys' range.
A patch here, a patch there, so absurd,
As silly whispers drift like birds.

The hedgehog sings a lullaby,
While bouncing jelly in the sky.
With rosy cheeks and laughter loud,
They form a wacky, happy crowd.

Let's stitch our dreams with candy threads,
In this kooky world where fun spreads.
For life's a quilt of daring seams,
So grab your needles, sew your dreams!

Horizons of the Imagination

In a land where socks can fly,
And giggles float on by,
The trees wear hats of every hue,
While rabbits brew some carrot stew.

Cats in boots spin tales of old,
While mice dance daring, brave, and bold.
A sky that rainbows up and down,
The sun dons shades, a golden crown.

With each new thought, a kite takes flight,
Whirling whimsies in the light.
A parade of dreams, colorful and grand,
As jellybeans scatter across the land.

Laughter echoes, sweet and clear,
Cucumbers dressed as engineers.
In this realm where silliness reigns,
Imagination knows no chains.

A Bouquet of Whimsical Thoughts

In a garden where oddities bloom,
Where toasters sing to chase the gloom.
Tulips wear polka-dot socks, oh my!
And daisies gossip while butterflies fly.

Lemonade rivers flow with glee,
As candy canes form a twisted tree.
The sun throws confetti, a brilliant splash,
While pastries invite you to have a bash.

Giggling mushrooms tap-dance in rows,
With jelly-filled clouds that jiggle and pose.
A bouquet of thoughts, peculiarly bright,
In the land of the wacky, all feels just right.

As rain falls cupcakes from the sky,
And gummy bears leap, oh so spry.
In this peculiar infinity, we weave,
Every chuckle is something to believe.

The Gatekeepers of Hidden Futures

Locksmiths of dreams with a twisty key,
Guard oddities that no one can see.
With a wink and a nod, they disclose,
The secrets hidden beneath your nose.

Frogs in suits hold meetings at night,
While stars twirl like dancers, oh what a sight!
They keep watch over wishes like treasure chests,
And bubblegum clouds pass the whimsical tests.

A raccoon in glasses reads fortune each day,
While clock hands tick-tock and say hooray!
In this kingdom of giggles, all feels so right,
Where hidden futures shine oh so bright.

With a tap on your shoulder, a laugh on the breeze,
The gatekeepers share secrets with amusing teas.
You'll never know what tomorrow will gleam,
For life is a canvas, painted with dream.

Learning to Dance with Shadows

Shadows giggle and tease under the trees,
As moonbeams whisper like a gentle breeze.
With bright socks on, they sway and spin,
In a hallway of laughter, where all can win.

Learning to cha-cha with bouncy sprites,
Through fuzzy dreams and starlit nights.
They trip over giggles, and tumble with glee,
As shadows weave stories, wild and free.

In ticklish corners, they hide and seek,
Planting silly secrets with every peek.
A dance of the whimsical, shadowy and light,
Where each little twirl brings joy to the night.

Join in their revelry, don't hesitate,
Take a leap into dreams, they await.
With laughter as music, take your sweet chance,
For in this fun world, we all must dance.

Underneath a Canopy of Stars

Beneath the winks of cosmic eyes,
We dance with hopes that laugh and rise.
A cheeky comet zips right by,
Tickling dreams as they float sky high.

The moon joins in with a goofy grin,
Whispering secrets on a whim.
Shooting stars race with silly glee,
In the night, we plot our spree.

Galaxies spin like a jolly tune,
As we burst forth like a bright balloon.
Constellations tease with a playful jest,
In this sky, we seek our quest.

With every twinkle, laughter gleams,
We chase the shadows of our dreams.
Under this sky, come laugh with me,
In the vastness, we're wild and free.

A Tapestry of Luminous Visions

In a weave of light, we find our fate,
With threads of whimsy and laughter great.
Each stitch a giggle, each knot a cheer,
Creating visions that feel so near.

Colors swirl like ice cream on a cone,
Delicious dreams we can call our own.
With every twist, a chuckle springs,
In this fabric, joy forever clings.

A splash of orange, a hint of blue,
The patterns dance, a comedic view.
We thread our tales with humor bright,
Crafting stories that take flight.

With a wink and nudge from fate's own hand,
We stitch our laughter, a giggling band.
In this tapestry, we'll boldly soar,
Creating magic forevermore.

The Archway of Infinite Possibilities

Step through the arch with a skip and hop,
Into a realm where silliness won't stop.
With each new door that creaks ajar,
Oddities await, oh how bizarre!

A garden of giggles, a plant that sings,
With fruits of laughter and zany things.
Here, shadows paint the walls with cheer,
Inviting all to laugh and leer.

Beneath the arch, the world feels bright,
Every path glows with pure delight.
You might trip over whimsy's feet,
But laughter, my friend, is oh so sweet!

Through every opening, a joke will bloom,
Filling every corner of every room.
So saunter on and don't be shy,
In this archway, let your spirit fly!

Winding Roads of the Mind

On winding roads where thoughts run free,
Silly ideas branch like a tree.
With twists and turns, a chuckle blooms,
Filling corners, brightening glooms.

A detour leads to a pratfall scene,
Where clowns parade in a world so keen.
We trip on dreams, we tumble and play,
In our minds, we dance all day.

Some paths are tricky, some lead to joy,
Like a child with a brightly wrapped toy.
Every thought is a step so bold,
Creating laughter as we unfold.

Crossroads beckon with playful grins,
Where absurdity starts and reason spins.
So join the ride, let's laugh and unwind,
On these winding roads of the mind.

Threads Woven in Starlight.

In a closet of socks, a dream took flight,
Chasing after shadows in the pale moonlight.
Old cat yawns wide, a magician's flair,
As I trip on my shoes, with no time to spare.

A ladder of noodles leads to the moon,
Where spaghetti strands dance to a silly tune.
My pet goldfish naps, plotting his escape,
While I juggle my thoughts, in a tinfoil cape.

The toaster hums softly, a musical muse,
As the closet door creaks, giving me the blues.
A pickle for wisdom, a donut for cheer,
In this carnival dreamland, I hold dear.

With giggling clouds and a twinkling star,
This faraway land is never too far.
For laughter is woven in every bright seam,
In this zany world, we all chase a dream.

Whispers of the Starry Night

The stars in the sky are a bit out of touch,
They laugh at my jokes, say I'm just too much.
A pizza slice flies, oh what a delight,
As I dance with the moon in my fuzzy white tights.

A cheeseburger comet blazes up high,
While donuts on clouds frolic and fly.
I twirl with the breeze, sharing secrets with trees,
And giggle at shadows that tickle my knees.

The moon's got a smile, a mischievous grin,
As I count all my socks—found one in the bin!
The stars wink and whisper, "Don't take life too tight,"
In a world full of wonder, just savor the night.

So here's to the chaos, the laughter, the cheer,
As I bounce on a comet, shout "I'm still here!"
With a sprinkle of stardust, my dreams take their flight,
In this whimsical, wacky, starry night!

Garden of Forgotten Wishes

In a garden of giggles, I planted my dreams,
Where marshmallow bushes sprout silly extremes.
The flowers all sway, wearing hats made of jam,
Whispering secrets to soft, chubby lambs.

A peppered pickle sits under the sun,
Wishing for laughter, just trying to have fun.
Old shoes as planters sprout daisies and peas,
All buzzing with joy, like a ticklish breeze.

I water my hopes with lemonade streams,
As shadows do the cha-cha, or so it seems.
The moon peeks through, wearing roller skates,
While fireflies mug for a giggle-filled fate.

Every inch of this garden, a dance full of cheer,
With candy cane trees, it's the place to be clear.
Where wishes are whispered to grow without bounds,
In this whimsical wonder where laughter resounds.

Shadows in the Moonlight

Beneath the moon's glow, my shadow does prance,
A whimsical ghost in a wobbly dance.
The owl hoots a joke, but it's not very clear,
As I tickle the wind with a giggle and cheer.

Losing my shoes in the fun of the night,
As shadows play tag, igniting delight.
The stars are a chorus, singing with glee,
While I twirl through the grass, as free as can be.

The glow from the moon drapes a silly cape,
With firefly friends, I'm escaping the drape.
A chocolate fountain spills wisdom, they say,
In this playful world where laughter holds sway.

So here in the shadows, the mischief is grand,
I dance with my shadow, together we stand.
In this moonlit laughter, there's nothing so bright,
As the shadows that play in the soft, silvery night.

Through the Eyes of the Dreamer

In a world where socks can fly,
Chasing butterflies up high,
Pigs wear hats, and cows can sing,
What joy such nonsense can bring!

With marshmallow clouds in the sky,
And jellybeans rolling by,
We dance on rainbows, oh so bright,
And laugh with gnomes in pure delight!

Counting sheep, we run the race,
But they all trip and lose their pace,
In a leap, we join the play,
Giggling all the livelong day!

As night falls down, the stars appear,
Winking at us, oh so near,
In a dreamer's world, we're the kings,
Crafting joy from silly things!

The Labyrinth of Aspirations

In a maze of wishes, we get lost,
Giant cheese and jelly, at what cost?
We trade our dreams for shiny toys,
And ride on flamingos, oh what joys!

Navigating paths with rubber shoes,
Finding clues in candy clues,
The hedgehogs cheer us on our quest,
While penguins come to put us to rest!

Around each corner, jokes abound,
Silly whispers, laughter found,
We twirl on capes made out of fluff,
In this wacky world, we can't get enough!

So when the road makes you detour,
Remember laughter is the cure,
In the labyrinth where dreams can roam,
We build our castle, we call it home!

Fragrant Trails of Memory

With scents of vanilla and fresh-baked pie,
We travel down lanes where memories fly,
Marshmallow forests and cookie streams,
Here, nothing's as it seems!

A dragon sneezes, out comes a cake,
Elves giggle hard, for goodness' sake!
We ride on cupcakes, through sprinkles and cheer,
In this sweet realm, we have no fear!

Collecting giggles in jars on the way,
As humor mounts, and shadows play,
The clocks tick backwards, we dance the jig,
With snappy turtles, oh so big!

So let us wander, through fragrance and fun,
Where laughter's a journey, and joy's never done,
With trails of memory that twist and turn,
In this fragrant land, there's so much to learn!

When Stars Bloom in Silence

When the sun sleeps and shadows creep,
The stars awaken, secrets to keep,
Bouncing on clouds, in a sleepy parade,
Wizards in pajamas, such plans they've made!

A giggle here, a chuckle there,
Moonbeams playing with silver hair,
Turtles twirl in the cosmic dance,
All caught up in this starry romance!

Nighttime whispers, stories unfold,
Of flying fish and marzipan gold,
We ride on comets, oh so bright,
Chasing our wishes into the night!

As laughter twinkles in nooks of the sky,
To these silly dreams, we can't say goodbye,
For when stars bloom soft in the moon's gentle light,
We find pure joy in the quiet of night!

Threads of Enchanted Hope

In a garden where wishes sway,
A snail claimed it was the next big play.
He donned a hat, quite out of style,
Promised the world with a cheeky smile.

A cat in glasses offered advice,
On how to roll dice made of rice.
With every toss, hope floated high,
As birds chirped tunes about pie in the sky.

A frog held court atop a log,
Declared he'd dance while hiding a fog.
His moves were wild, like popcorn in heat,
All the bugs cheered for his vibrant beat.

So in this space of slightly mad schemes,
We gather our fears and weave our dreams.
For laughter is magic, a sweet little thread,
Tying us closer, where mischief is spread.

Paths Worn by Barefoot Desires

On pathways painted with candy rain,
Kids run barefoot, screaming in fun gain.
A bumblebee wore a tiny crown,
Buzzed about gossip from town to town.

The flowers giggled, showing their stripes,
As ants paraded with spectacular types.
They clambered together, just trying to find,
What treasure was hidden, their hearts intertwined.

A shoelace tied a shoe to a worm,
Together they spun, in a whimsical term.
With laughter erupting like fizzy soda,
They raced through the grass, avoiding the colder.

So here we dance on paths of pure joy,
With each little stumble, we giggle, oh boy!
Let's shed our worries, embrace silly sights,
For barefoot adventures are wild, full of lights.

The Lattice of Fantasies

In a land where clouds wear funky hats,
Ducks print newspapers while chatting like cats.
They report on the latest mud pie wars,
While pine trees dance, revealing their chores.

A jester fox juggles his dreams made of cheese,
While squirrels debate what kind of tree please.
They laugh at the moon as it trips on a star,
In this playful hive, we all go bizarre.

A rainbow slides down a slippery hill,
Whispers of giggles linger, quiet and still.
With each twist and turn, the colors collide,
Creating a canvas where joy can reside.

So join this jolly, enchanted charade,
Where laughter is currency, brightly displayed.
As fantasies bloom and whimsies are spun,
In this world of wonder, we can all be young.

A Canvas of Celestial Visions

Stars painted polka dots on the sky,
While comets zoomed by, just daring to fly.
A curious cloud wore a tutu, quite grand,
Twisting and swirling, struck by a hand.

In this gallery where giggles are art,
A painter named Luna has captured the heart.
She splashes the cosmos with bubbles of cheer,
And moons play tag as their friends disappear.

With each brushstroke, a new tale unfolds,
Of aliens hula-hooping, bold and quite bold.
They spin through the night, causing stars to collide,
Sharing secrets of dancing from planets they'd bide.

So swirl in this world of whimsical dreams,
Where laughter echoes and sunlight beams.
For a canvas of visions can tickle and tease,
Inviting us all to join in with ease.

The Alchemy of Wishes

In a pot of giggles, wishes brew,
With laughter's spice, a funny stew.
Stir in a pickle, add a slice of cheese,
Why not make a wish that tickles your knees?

A twirl of whimsy, a dash of flair,
Socks mismatched, but who would care?
Sprinkle some bubbles, watch them fly,
Wishes made, but don't ask why!

Dance like a chicken, sing like a cat,
Inflation of dreams—imagine that!
With every tumble, dreams sway and weave,
In this funny world, we truly believe.

So gather your since and fill up the cup,
Pour in the giggles, don't let them stop.
For in this alchemy, we've found the key,
To turn life's nonsense into a spree!

Journey of the Wandering Soul

A soul in slippers, wandering free,
In search of snacks and a cup of tea.
With every step, a trail of cheer,
Chasing after thoughts—oh dear, oh dear!

The clouds are fluffy, a cotton candy,
Falling on heads—this journey is dandy!
From pizza trees to rivers of jam,
Life's a talent show; just be the clown!

With a wink and a giggle, off we go,
Dodging the chores and the daily woe.
A map made of gummy bears in hand,
Each sticky step is totally unplanned!

So skip and leap through the fields of fun,
Embrace the folly, don't let it run.
The journey's silly, but oh-so-bright,
Every wandering soul deserves delight!

Orchestrating Stars in a Jar

A jar of stars, oh what a mess,
Tangled twinkles, I must confess.
I tried to catch them for a dance,
But they just giggled and took a chance!

With fireflies laughing, I set the stage,
Crickets chirping, it's all the rage.
A symphony of whimsy in the night,
But all they do is wobble and bite!

So I tickled the lid and gave a wink,
And stars started dancing on the brink.
They spun and twirled, with glee untamed,
In a joyful jam, they happily claimed.

With a pluck and a strum, the moon took a bow,
In this jar of dreams, we didn't know how.
To orchestrate laughter, a cosmos of glee,
In this polka-dot jar, we're all fancy and free!

The Silk Thread of Possibility

A thread of silk, all shiny and bright,
Wove a tapestry of pure delight.
I pulled on it gently, and lo and behold,
Out popped a cat that was wearing pure gold!

With every tug, a new tale unfolds,
A pickle that dances, a fish made of folds.
Unravel the wonders, let laughter reign,
In the threads of whimsy, there's never a pain!

Stitching together the odd and the grand,
A snail in a top hat, a condiment band.
We sew with our dreams, wrapped in a chuckle,
Each knot a reminder of joy's endless buckle.

So spin that silk, let the colors collide,
In the fabric of laughter, we take our ride.
For in this cozy quilt stitched with glee,
The silk thread of possibility sets us all free!

Symphony of Unspoken Yearnings

In the quiet of a bustling mind,
We dance to tunes that are hard to find.
Whispers of hopes in a chorus of glee,
Juggling our wishes like clowns at the sea.

A cat sketches plans with a twirl of its tail,
While shoes sashay forth with a curious trail.
Odd socks unite in a quirky parade,
Each dreaming of worlds where they won't be dismayed.

An umbrella dreams of stars up above,
While a teapot hums of unspilled love.
Lemonade rivers and cake on a boat,
Sailors dream bigger on seas made of oat.

So let's frolic in laughter, with whims at our side,
For the heart's true desires are often so spry.
With giggles as anchors, we'll sway with the breeze,
Unraveling futures, a comical tease.

Where Dreams Take Root

In a garden where wishes sprout from the ground,
The cucumbers giggle, their giggle profound.
While carrots wear hats and dance in a line,
Stepping to rhythms of sunlight and wine.

A tomato turns red at the stroke of noon,
Reciting old fables to the bright, silver moon.
The radishes chuckle as they peek from the dirt,
Trading their secrets with each little spurt.

Woolly clouds gather, with laughter they taunt,
As the daisies spin tales that no one can flaunt.
The sunflower bows to the rhythm of glee,
Where dreams take root, wild and carefree.

Butterflies whisper, "Let's dance through the skies,"
Tickling petals with giggles and sighs.
A harvest of laughter awaits on the floor,
Where dreams find their roots, and so much more!

Petals of Midnight Dreams

As night draws its curtain, we burst into song,
Starlit giggles twirl, it won't be long.
Whispers of joy waft through the air,
Petals of wishes, tangled without a care.

Kittens conspire with socks in a heap,
Dreaming of lands where they dance in their sleep.
Balloons giggle wildly as they float up high,
Comically seeking a piece of the pie.

The lamps are winking, their light soft and bold,
Sharing tall tales of the brave and the old.
A sandwich chuckles while resting on plates,
Spinning grand stories of love and of fates.

So grab your own flower, let laughter take flight,
In gardens of whimsy, where dreams turn to light.
Through petals of midnight, we joyfully prance,
Yielding to magic, we merrily dance!

The Frame of Distant Horizons

With a flick of a brush on horizons afar,
We sketch silly things, like a dog with a car.
Mountains of ice cream pierce the blue sky,
While sprinkles rain down with a soft, happy sigh.

A fox in a top hat takes lead in the play,
As clouds serenade in their puffy ballet.
Giraffes dressed in stripes tease the sun with delight,
Bouncing through puddles, tickling the night.

Lighthouse lit visions spin tales on the shore,
Frogs in fine suits go to dances galore.
Wishing stars giggle in elegant styles,
Painting mischief across countless miles.

So uncover the map to your faraway lands,
Where fun holds the compass, and laughter commands.
Let dreams fill your sails, steady and bright,
The frame of the world is a canvas of light.

www.ingramcontent.com/pod-product-compliance
Lightning Source LLC
Chambersburg PA
CBHW071853160426
43209CB00003B/537